Margot Richardson

Photographs by Chris Fairclough

CHERRYTREE BOOKS

Distributed in the United States by
Cherrytree Books
1980 Lookout Drive
North Mankato, MN 56001

U.S. publication copyright © Cherrytree Books 2005
International copyright reserved in all countries. No part of
this book may be reproduced in any form without written
permission from the publisher.

Library of Congress Cataloging-in-Publication Data
Richardson, Margot.
    Australia / by Margot Richardson ; photographs by
Chris Fairclough.
        p. cm. -- (Letters from around the world)
    Includes bibliographical references (p.31) and index.
    ISBN 1-84234-245-2 (alk. paper)
     1. Australia--Juvenile literature. I. Fairclough, Chris.
    II. Title. III. Series.

DU96.R535 2004
994--dc22

                            2004041307

First Edition
9 8 7 6 5 4 3 2 1

First published in 2004 by
Evans Brothers Ltd
2A Portman Mansions
Chiltern Street
London W1U 6NR
Copyright © Evans Brothers 2004

Conceived and produced by

Nutshell
MEDIA

www.nutshellmedialtd.co.uk

Editor: Katie Orchard
Design: Mayer Media Ltd
Cartography: Encompass Graphics Ltd
Artwork: Tim Mayer
Consultants: Jeff Stanfield and Anne Spiring

All photographs were taken by Chris Fairclough.

Printed in China

Acknowledgments
The authors would like to thank the Hulme family, and
the principal, staff, and students of Stanmore Public
School, Sydney, for all their help with this book.

Cover: Harriet with her brother Nicholas and friends
    Victoria and Max, in front of the Sydney Harbour
Bridge.
Title page: Harriet and her friend Olivia belong to a surf
    lifeguard club at Bondi Beach.
This page: A view over the center of Sydney.
Contents page: Harriet holds a pumpkin she has grown.
Glossary page: Harriet and her dad meet a koala at the zoo.
Further information page: Harriet's class works on a project
    about Aborigines.
Index: Harriet has a horseback riding lesson.

Contents

My Country

Saturday, January 3

33 Boronia Street
Stanmore
Sydney
NSW 2048
Australia

Dear Jo,

G'day! (This is how some Australians say hello. It's short for "Good day.")

My name is Harriet Hulme and I'm nine years old. I live with my family in Sydney, the biggest city in Australia. I have two sisters, Kate, who's 12, and Charlotte, who's five. I also have a brother, Nicholas, who's seven. I can't wait to help you with your school project on Australia.

Write back soon!

From
Harriet ↗

Here's my family. I'm in front (in the red top) with Nicholas. In the back, from left to right, are Mom, Charlotte, Dad, and Kate.

Australia is a huge island, called a continent. Most Australians live on the strip of coast that starts at Melbourne and runs up past Sydney to Brisbane.

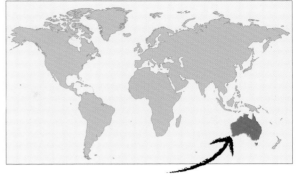

Australia's place in the world.

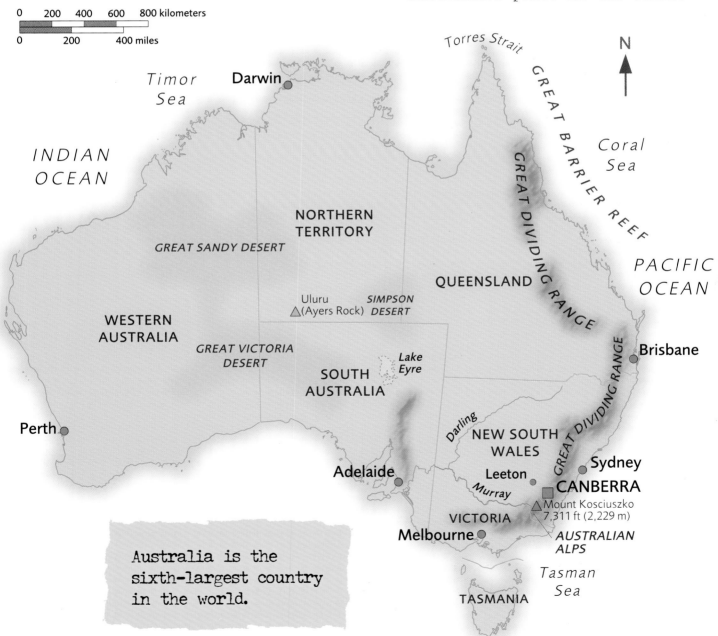

Australia is the sixth-largest country in the world.

The center of Sydney was built around a large, natural harbor. The first people to live there were the Aborigines, Australia's indigenous people.

In 1788, people from Britain arrived in ships and started to build a small town. Over the next 200 years, Sydney grew into a busy, modern city. Now, more than four million people live there.

Sydney's famous landmark is the Opera House. Its roof looks like the sails of a ship.

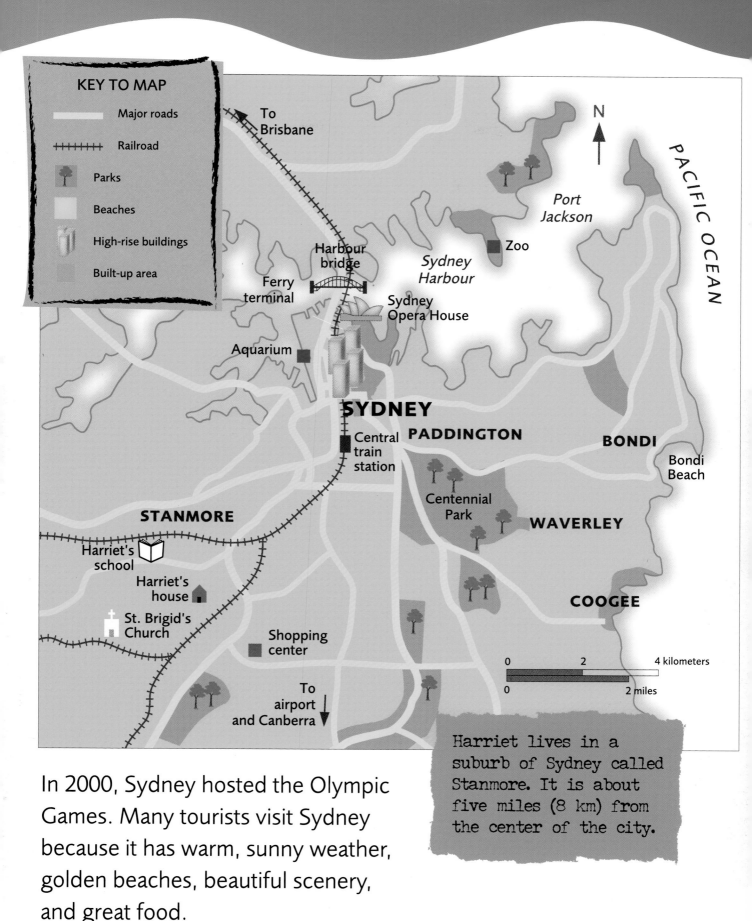

KEY TO MAP

——— Major roads

+++++++ Railroad

Parks

Beaches

High-rise buildings

Built-up area

To Brisbane

N

PACIFIC OCEAN

Port Jackson

Zoo

Sydney Harbour

Harbour bridge

Ferry terminal

Sydney Opera House

Aquarium

SYDNEY

Central train station

PADDINGTON

BONDI

Bondi Beach

Centennial Park

WAVERLEY

STANMORE

Harriet's school

Harriet's house

COOGEE

St. Brigid's Church

Shopping center

0   2   4 kilometers

0   2 miles

To airport and Canberra

In 2000, Sydney hosted the Olympic Games. Many tourists visit Sydney because it has warm, sunny weather, golden beaches, beautiful scenery, and great food.

Harriet lives in a suburb of Sydney called Stanmore. It is about five miles (8 km) from the center of the city.

Landscape and Weather

The east coast of Australia is warm and wet. The center of the country is desert, and it is mostly hot and dry. The north is very hot and humid, and has fierce storms called cyclones. In the south there are mountains called the Australian Alps, where it snows in winter.

Harriet and her friend, Olivia, belong to a surf lifeguard club. They wear special caps so they can be seen easily in the sea.

In Sydney the hottest months are December, January, and February, and the coolest are July and August.

Most Australians live by the coast. Bondi Beach, in Sydney, is the perfect place for relaxing and surfing in the waves.

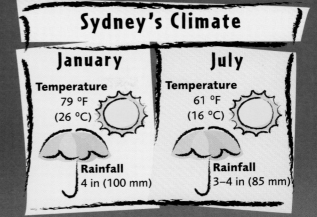

Sydney's Climate

January

Temperature
79 ºF
(26 ºC)

Rainfall
4 in (100 mm)

July

Temperature
61 ºF
(16 ºC)

Rainfall
3–4 in (85 mm)

At Home

Like most people in Sydney, Harriet's family lives in a house with a yard. Stanmore is one of the older parts of Sydney. Many of the houses here were built more than 100 years ago, which is quite old for Australia.

Harriet's house has a **veranda**, which gives shade in hot weather.

Harriet's house has four bedrooms, two bathrooms, a living room, a dining room, a kitchen, and a study, which Harriet's dad uses for work.

Harriet sometimes reads to Charlotte before they go to bed.

Harriet shares a bedroom with her sister Charlotte. Kate and Nicholas each have a room of their own.

Harriet's family plays a board game in the living room.

The back yard is just big enough to fit in a trampoline.

Harriet's house is near the center of the city, so the yard is not very big. A lot of the houses farther away from the city center have large yards. Many houses even have space for a swimming pool.

Harriet feeds her pet cat, Tigger, in the garden.

Friday, April 17

33 Boronia Street
Stanmore
Sydney
NSW 2048
Australia

Dear Jo,

I enjoyed reading about your house. We have a vegetable patch in our garden. We grow tomatoes, carrots, spinach, broccoli, beets, corn, pumpkins, and some herbs. In summer, when it's really hot, we have to water them every day.

I like the pumpkins best. They have a hard skin and are orange and sweet inside. We eat pumpkin with a roast dinner, mashed like potatoes, or made into soup. It's yummy!

From

Harriet

Pumpkins grow on a vine. This one is big and heavy, but it's not ripe yet.

Food and Mealtimes

For breakfast, Harriet usually has cereal with milk, toast with a yeast spread called Vegemite, and some fruit juice.

Harriet takes a packed lunch to school. She has a honey or Vegemite sandwich, some fruit, a drink and homemade cookies or cakes.

On warm mornings, Harriet's family eats breakfast outside in the garden.

Australian people used to eat mainly plain meat with vegetables. Now foods from all around the world are popular.

In the evenings, Harriet's family may have pasta, a stir-fry with chicken, roast lamb, or fish and chips.

Harriet's mom buys most of the family's food at the supermarket.

On most evenings, the family eats dinner together in the dining room.

Harriet's family has
a Chinese meal in
Sydney's Chinatown.

On special days, such as
birthdays, Harriet's family
eats out in a restaurant.
There is a huge choice
of restaurants: Thai,
Vietnamese, Chinese,
Greek, Italian, African,
and Indian.

In the summer, the
family sometimes has a
barbecue in the garden.

Sunday, June 14

33 Boronia Street
Stanmore
Sydney
NSW 2048
Australia

Dear Jo,

You asked for a typical Australian recipe. Here's how to make Anzac cookies. We often make them.

You will need: $3/4$ cup rolled oats, 1 cup flour, $3/4$ cup sugar, $1/2$ cup dried coconut, 1 tablespoon molasses, 1 stick butter, $1/2$ teaspoon baking soda, 1 tablespoon very hot water.

1. Mix the oats, flour, sugar, and coconut in a large bowl.
2. Ask an adult to help melt the molasses and butter in a pan.
3. Mix together the soda and water. Add the butter and molasses.
4. Add this to the dry mixture in the bowl, and mix well.
5. Place tablespoonfuls of the mixture on the greased cookie sheet.
6. Bake in the oven at 300 °F for 20 minutes.

I hope you like them!

From

Harriet

Here I am putting balls of the cookie mixture on to a cookie sheet. →

School Day

Harriet goes to a school near her home. It takes about five minutes to get there by car. There are 420 boys and girls at Harriet's school, from 5 to 12 years old.

At Harriet's school, everyone wears a school uniform, including a special hat to protect them from the sun.

There are 30 children
in Harriet's class.
They are having a
reading lesson.

In Harriet's art class,
the children learn
about Aboriginal
paintings, and try the
style for themselves.

School starts with assembly at 9 A.M. and finishes at 3 P.M. Harriet studies English, math, science and technology, drama, history, geography, scripture, music, art, and sports. Harriet's favorite subject is drama.

There are 10 computers in Harriet's classroom and a computer center in the school library.

Some of these children are playing cricket on the school playground.

Harriet's school has three playgrounds and a grassy playing field. The children play softball (which is a bit like baseball), cricket, volleyball, and soccer.

On warm afternoons after school, Harriet does her homework outside.

Some children have after-school classes. They sing in the choir, or play in the school band. Others learn ballet or tennis.

Monday, September 14

33 Boronia Street
Stanmore
Sydney
NSW 2048
Australia

Dear Jo,

Ni Hao! (pronounced "nee how." It means "hello!" in Mandarin.)

There are many people from other countries living in Australia. The three main groups living in our area speak Greek, Mandarin, or Portuguese. Each week, everyone in our school has a lesson to study the different countries and their languages. Sometimes, we cook some of their foods or learn traditional dances.

Are you learning any other languages?

From

Harriet

This is my Mandarin class. Mandarin is one of the languages spoken in China.

Off to Work

Harriet's mum is a deputy principal at a high school. She works all day, from 8:30 A.M. to 5:30 P.M.

Harriet's dad is a veterinarian. He has a shorter working day so that he can pick up the children from school and be with them at home in the afternoons.

Harriet's dad works with animals to keep them healthy.

Some of the trains that take people to work in Sydney have double-decker carriages. This means that more people can fit onto one train.

In Sydney, many people work in offices, stores, and restaurants. They travel to work by car, or on trains that take people in and out of the center of the city.

These Italian women run a pizza restaurant near Harriet's home.

Free Time

When all Harriet's schoolwork is done, she likes reading, playing with her friends, and watching television. She also goes swimming, plays netball, and rides her bike.

Koalas are native Australian animals. It is hard to find them in the wild, so most people see them in zoos.

Harriet has lessons to improve her riding. She always wears a helmet to protect her head if she falls.

Harriet's grandparents live on a farm about a seven-hour drive from Sydney. During the school vacation, the whole family goes to stay there. When Harriet is visiting her grandparents, she enjoys horseback riding.

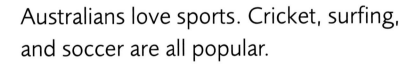

Australians love sports. Cricket, surfing, and soccer are all popular.

These people are playing a game of touch rugby on the beach while others swim and surf in the sea behind.

25

Religion and Festivals

Most Australians are Christian, but many of them do not often go to church. Harriet's family is Catholic. On Sunday mornings, Harriet and her mom go to their local church, called St. Brigid's.

A Sunday morning mass at St. Brigid's Church, where Harriet goes with her mother.

Greek and Chinese Christians have their own churches. There are also many Buddhist centers and temples in Sydney.

On Easter, Greek Christians have a parade, to mark the day that Jesus rose from the dead.

Wednesday, December 29

33 Boronia Street
Stanmore
Sydney
NSW 2048
Australia

Dear Jo,

Thanks for my Christmas card! In Australia, Christmas comes during our long summer vacation. Even though it's hot outside, we still put up Christmas trees and have decorations with pretend snow!

This year we spent Christmas Day at home and had a traditional roast turkey dinner with plum pudding for desert. Last year, we were at my grandparents' farm, where we celebrated with my dad's huge family—there were 43 of us! It was 100 °F (40 °C) outside, so we had an Australian lunch of shrimp, cold meats, and salads.

From

Harriet

This is me finding my presents under the tree on Christmas morning. I was given a portable CD player, a board game, and a new boogie board and flippers.

Fact File

Capital City: Canberra is a modern city that was specially built for Australia's national parliament.

Other major cities: Sydney, Melbourne, Brisbane and Perth.

Size: 2,954,825 square miles (7,686,850 km²).

Population: 19,600,000

Indigenous Population: The first Australians, the Aborigines and Torres Strait Islanders, have lived in Australia for about 50,000 years. They make up two percent of Australia's population. (The first European people settled in Australia just over 200 years ago.)

Flag: Australia's flag includes the Union flag, to show that Australia is part of the British Commonwealth. It also has five white stars to show the Southern Cross, a pattern of stars that can be seen in the Australian sky. The large, seven-pointed star represents the states and territories of Australia.

Currency: The Australian dollar, made up of 100 cents.

Main Religions: Christianity. Other religions include Islam, Buddhism, Judaism, and Hinduism.

Stamps: Australian stamps often show native animals, plants, and flowers, like the ones below. Others have photos of landscapes, sports, festivals, and famous Australians.

Languages: English is the main language. However, 24 percent of the people living in Australia were born in other countries, or have parents from other countries. The other languages spoken most are Italian, Greek, Cantonese, Arabic, and Vietnamese.

Main Industries: Manufacturing (food and machinery) are big industries, and so are business and finance. Agriculture and coal mining are also important.

Longest River: Murray River 1,605 miles (2,589 km).

Highest Mountain: Mount Kosciuszko, 7,311 feet (2,229 m). It is found in the Australian Alps, in southern New South Wales.

Australian Wildlife: Most of Australia's native animals are not found in any other countries. These include animals that raise their young in pouches on their bodies, such as the koala, kangaroo (shown below), and possum. Others are the only mammals that lay eggs, the platypus and the echidna.

Glossary

Anzac Anzac stands for Australia and New Zealand Army Corps, which was the force that fought in World War I. Anzac cookies were named after these soldiers because Australians were very proud of them.

Aborigines The first people who lived in Australia. They were the only people living there until people from Britain settled in 1788.

Christian Someone who follows the teachings of Jesus Christ.

continent A big, continuous expanse of land. Europe, Africa, Asia, North America, South America, Australasia, and Antarctica are continents.

cyclone A fierce storm with very strong winds.

desert Dry land with very little water.

harbor A place on a coast where ships can shelter.

humid Damp or moist.

indigenous Coming from a particular place. This is the word that Australian Aborigines use to describe themselves.

native A plant or animal that was born in, or belongs to, a particular place.

scripture The Australian name for learning about religion, mainly Christianity.

stir fry A way of cooking where meat and vegetables are cut into small pieces and fried quickly. Chinese and Thai foods are often cooked in this way.

suburbs The areas on the edges of a city, where most people live.

surf Waves breaking on a beach.

Vegemite A type of dark, salty spread made from concentrated yeast extract. It is very popular in Australia.

veranda A roofed area on the outside of a house, usually on the ground floor.

Further Information

Information Books:

Fox, Mary. *Continents: Australia and Oceania*. Heinemann Library, 2003.

Richardson, Adele. *Let's investigate: Australia*. Creative Education, 1998.

Martin, Fred. *Next Stop Australia*. Heinemann Library, 1998.

Pluckrose, Henry. *Picture a Country: Australia*. Franklin Watts, 2001.

Fiction:

Morgan, Sally. *The Flying Emu and Other Australian Stories*. Knopf, 1993.

Web sites:

Australia
www.australia.com
Information for tourists.

Visit NSW
www.visitnsw.com.au
Information on New South Wales.

Aboriginal Art Online
www.aboriginalartonline.com/
Pictures of traditional and modern art by Aboriginal people.

Stanmore Public School
www.stanmore-p.schools.nsw.edu.au/
The web site of Harriet's school, including details of festivals celebrated and a kids' forum.

Zootopia
www.zo.nsw.gov.au
A zoo web site with information about native animals.

Index